Police Oral Boards

The Ultimate Guide to a Successful Oral Board Interview

Mark Denton

"I am the Officer"

I have been where you fear to be,
I have seen what you fear to see,
I have done what you fear to do -
All these things I have done for you.

I am the person you lean upon,
The one you cast your scorn upon,
The one you bring your troubles to -
All these people I've been for you.

The one you ask to stand apart,
The one you feel should have no heart,
The one you call "The Officer in Blue,"
But I'm just a person, just like you.

And through the years I've come to see,
That I am not always what you ask of me;
So, take this badge ... take this gun ...
Will you take it ... will anyone?

And when you watch a person die
And hear a battered baby cry,
Then do you think that you can be
All these things you ask of me?

(Author unknown)

ISBN-10: 1442157992

ISBN-13: 978-1442157996

Cover Design: Burnt Sky Media
www.burntskymedia.com

Contents

Introduction

In my past 15 + years as a police officer, there's one thing I learned for certain: jobs in law enforcement don't always go to the most qualified individuals—they go to the most prepared. And now, there is finally a guide dedicated solely to helping you prepare for and successfully pass the ultra-competitive law enforcement oral board interview.

Yes, you can definitely find countless books on preparing for the written test in law enforcement and even more books on the topic of preparing for a job interview, but very few, if any, can be found specifically dealing with the all important oral board interview.

Ask anyone who has ever participated in a law enforcement testing process and they are sure to tell you that it's one of the most difficult things they have ever done. And if you were to dig a little deeper, you'll also find that it is the dreaded oral board interview that is by far the most difficult part of the law enforcement hiring process...and likely one of the most stressful events of their lives.

The oral board interview can make or break your chance at getting hired at the agency you want. For many, the oral board is a challenging experience, but with the right preparation, you can be successful in this portion of the testing process. Having the right information going into your oral board interview can lead to more confidence and this confidence is a necessary ingredient to a successful interview.

For most law enforcement agencies across the country, a structured oral board or panel interview plays an important role in the hiring of new peace officers. In fact, many agencies rely on the oral board results by as much as 75% of the overall testing score in selecting new applicants. Therefore, if the agency you're applying to does incorporate the oral board interview as part of its selection process, you will want to place great importance on the information contained in this book.

When writing this guide, it was surely my desire to address every possible oral board question, but I quickly found out that this was an exercise in futility. Over the course of the past year, however, I spent hundreds of hours researching and comparing the questions being asked on oral board interviews in various law enforcement agencies across the country, to finally bring you The Ultimate Guide to a Successful Oral Board Interview.

In December 2008, there were over 15,000 unfilled law enforcement positions in the state of California alone! When you take this number and apply it across the rest of the country, there is no doubt that there are many law enforcement job opportunities available to you, no matter where you live. Keep in mind, however, that despite the number of available jobs, law enforcement agencies across the country are still very "choosey" as to who they let in their ranks.

The recent downturn in our economy has resulted in an increase in the number of applicants for police department positions across the country. People are realizing that government jobs are usually safer than their private counterparts in these recessionary times. And unlike just two years ago, when police departments were fighting for applicants, we are now getting more applicants than we can handle.

What this means to you, the police applicant, is that competition is growing fierce. To get ahead of the competition, you've got to get better prepared.

This guide will do that.

Adequate preparation for a career in law enforcement is guaranteed to take you a long, long way. And that is the basis of this guide—to help prepare you for the exciting field of law enforcement by getting you ready for the tough challenge of the oral board interview ahead.

Study up and have confidence in yourself. Good luck!

Understanding the Oral Board

For most law enforcement agencies across the country, the oral board interview has become standard for gaining employment. The simple reason for this is because law enforcement agencies are interested in hiring only those who can demonstrate that they are capable of performing the duties of an officer. Oral board interviews are the demonstration grounds as they allow for law enforcement agencies to see "first hand" whether or not their applicants can meet their specific criteria.

The purpose of the oral board interview is to assess certain attitudes, motivation, understanding of police work, problem-solving skills, and oral communication skills that cannot be measured by the written test alone.

Normally, an oral board panel is comprised of 3 "board members" who are trained to assess and score the answers you give during the oral board interview. These oral board panels are usually comprised of law enforcement personnel and a law enforcement supervisor employed by the agency for which you are applying. However, they can sometimes contain Human Resources personnel, psychologists or citizens of the community for which that agency serves. It is also common for a panel of "raters" to be monitored by human resource personnel to ensure the tests remain fair and standardized.

The questions presented during the oral board interview are usually written by or in consultation with a "subject matter expert" in the law enforcement field. This way, the questions asked of you can be attributed to being applicable to the job you are applying for. That is to say, police officers should be the ones writing the oral board questions regarding police work because police officers are the experts in police work. They should also be the ones supplying the answers that your answers will be compared to during scoring.

For most agencies, the oral board process has evolved significantly over the past decade. These days, the oral board takes on a formal, structured interview format with predetermined questions that are asked of each applicant. To keep the test standardized, the exact same questions will be asked in the exact same order for each and every applicant that the oral board panel interviews.

The purpose of standardization is to give each applicant the same chance to succeed or fail. Deviating from this structure can give unsuccessful applicants reason to challenge the oral board process, which could possibly lead to litigation and possible monetary awards to an applicant that was not given his "fair shake." Remember, the whole purpose of testing applicants is to provide a fair, objective, and valid method of predicting which applicants will most likely be successful in the field of law enforcement.

During the interview, questions presented to applicants can usually be repeated (if requested by the applicant) but they cannot be rephrased or paraphrased. Also, oral board members can only use information that is told to them; they cannot prompt you further and they cannot "dig" for your answers.

Tip Always remember that the board can ONLY use what you give them. That being said, you must know that it is important to answer every question to the best of your ability and to be painfully articulate when doing so. Never just assume the board knows what you are talking about. You've got to be clear.

Also, the oral board panel cannot legally ask you certain questions. Questions that are prohibited in a job interview include questions regarding your marital status, religious affiliation and political beliefs.

In the past, I have witnessed oral board panels that, in my opinion, go about the process in the wrong way. Instead of presenting the utmost professional demeaner amongst *every* panel member, I have seen that many times an oral board panel will have one member whose purpose is to "rattle" you through sneers, looks of disgust and headshakes of disappointment as you answer the board's questions. While I do not agree with these methods, understand that this may occur. Also understand, however, that if you do witness these types of actions, it is meant only to be a test to see if you will "crack" under the pressure, change your answer, or simply give up. So, if you do see something like I've described, do not waiver in your answer—continue on and realize that it is just a "game." Always stand firm on your answers and say what you are going to say with confidence and conviction.

Oral Board Scoring

Understand that law enforcement agencies have traditional beliefs and ideas of what makes a "good cop" and how a "good cop" should behave and present themselves to others. These ideas and beliefs will surely come into play when an officer is tasked with rating a prospective police officer.

Prior to interviewing prospective law enforcement candidates, the oral board panel will receive training and instruction on how to score the answers of the interviewees. Unlike the written test, there is normally not just one "right" answer.

Because the oral board panel is made up of human beings, you can expect the scoring to be somewhat subjective, although scores should generally be in the same "objective direction." That is to say that your answers should be similarly, but not necessarily exactly, scored in the same "range" by each of the panel members.

Prior to the interviews, the board members are each given a score sheet to complete on each applicant. This "rating form" or "score sheet" lists the areas to be rated. Each board member will keep their own score. It is at this point, I have seen remarkable differences with regards to scoring. In some agencies, it is common that once the interview is complete, the oral board panel will discuss and compare scores to ensure someone did not miss an important point. In other agencies, however, each board member will submit their scores to a third party (usually a human resources employee) without discussion. Regardless of what the agency does after the interview, the scores are then combined and averaged to give the applicant a final score for their oral board interview.

The following areas are some of the most typically scored core elements of the law enforcement oral board interview. These are scored throughout the test, regardless of what types of questions are being asked.

Attitude and Motivation:

- Applicants are rated on their attitude towards the police and on their desire to serve the public

- Applicants are rated on their motivation towards police work — applicants motivation should focus on serving the public rather than looking at a career in law enforcement as just another job

Understanding of Position:

- Applicants are rated on their understanding of law enforcement work — they demonstrate that they are familiar with both the "pros & cons" of police work

- Applicants should show that they have a firm grasp on the duties and responsibilities of being a sworn officer

- Applicants should indicate that they are taking a career in law enforcement seriously and that they have put adequate thought into the position prior to applying

Oral Communication Skills:

- Applicants are rated on their ability to organize thoughts and on their ability to express them in a clear, logical manner

- Applicants are rated on their ability to listen to others — to ascertain if they are able to accurately comprehend what others are saying or asking

- Applicants are rated on their ability to speak with clarity with regards to their use of the appropriate choice of words and grammatical form

Interpersonal Skills:

- Applicants are rated on their ability to consider and respect differing values, feelings, needs and viewpoints of others and in their ability to establish and maintain a cooperative working relationship with those that have differing viewpoints

Problem Solving Skills/Judgment:

- Applicants are rated on their ability to identify a problem presented and provide answers/solutions that are logical, reasonable and relevant to the question posed

- Applicants are rated on their ability to exercise sound judgment consistent with the police role

Keep in mind that in most oral boards these are the core elements that are being evaluated. However, every oral board interview is different and what they view as being important can vary drastically. That being said, you must also expect the board to rate you on your perceived level of confidence, your integrity level, your maturity level, and your personal appearance and poise, amongst other things.

Oral Board Interview Format

If you are selected to participate in an oral board interview, you will be given a date, time and location for that interview. Upon arriving to your interview, you will be required to check-in. Make sure you do not just arrive and sit there. Make sure you let someone know that you are there so that the oral board does not think you arrived late.

In almost every instance, the oral board panel will be behind schedule and you will likely be required to wait a while before your interview starts.

When it is your turn, the Chairperson of the oral board will come outside to greet you and bring you into the interview room. Once in the room, you will be introduced to the other oral board panel members and anyone else present in the room.

Tip Upon being introduced with the board members, be sure to shake each of their hands with a firm handshake and try as best you can to "catch" and remember their names. Almost no one can recall the names after being told because there are so many other things clogging your head during the oral board interview. Also, do not sit down until someone tells you to take a seat. They will direct you where to sit.

After introductions, the board members will explain the process and the "rules" of the interview. Normally, these "rules" will be about time limits on answering questions, listening carefully, asking for questions to be repeated, etc.

During the interview, you will notice that the board members will take turns asking you questions. Additionally, you will notice that they will be taking notes as you answer questions posed of you. This is all completely normal—notes will be taken whether you say something "good" or "bad" so you need not be alarmed if you see someone writing while you speak.

> **Tip** Always sit up straight and be attentive when the board is asking you questions. Be sure to make good eye contact and be cognizant of your body language.

After the ground rules are established, the oral board panel will normally try to establish rapport with you and ask typical "ice breaker" type questions such as, "Tell us a little about yourself."

After the "ice breaker," the interview will progress into personal questions regarding your preparation, experience, desires, etc about becoming a law enforcement officer.

After these personal questions, the interview, in most cases, will go into situational/judgment type questions. These are normally conducted by presenting typical police scenarios and asking you how you would handle each.

After the situational/scenario questions, typically you will be asked what I call "willingness" questions. These questions will delve into your willingness to perform required duties of police work. For example, are you willing to work nights and weekends? Are you wiling to take a life if necessary?

Finally, most oral board interviews are concluded by the board asking you if you would like to add anything to the interview.

> **Tip**In my experience, most applicants are so happy to be done with their interview at this point, that they tell the board that there is nothing they would like to add, while they scurry out of the interview room as fast as they can. However, you should always take this opportunity to not only thank the oral board for their time, but you should also use the time to "sell" yourself as best you can. Let the board know how excited you are for the opportunity...tell them that you are ready to do whatever it takes to succeed. Reiterate some "selling points" about yourself prior to leaving the interview.

At the conclusion of the interview, you will be thanked for your time and they will let you know when you will receive your score/ranking. Some departments will quickly score your results on the spot, while others will send you the results in the mail. I have seen both methods equally applied across the country.

Advance Preparation — The Key to Success

For most applicants, the oral board interview is the most challenging portion of the hiring process. However, with the right preparation, you can be very successful. Proper research, demonstrable preparation, job knowledge and practice are key ingredients to ensuring yourself a successful oral board interview. These ingredients can lead you to more confidence and once again, confidence plays a major role in a successful oral board interview.

In this chapter, I will explain each of these key elements in detail.

First things first...

Understand that the law enforcement agency that is interviewing you is looking for someone who is seeking a career in law enforcement — not just another job. In that respect, they are going to want to know two things right off the bat:

1. Why do you want a career in law enforcement?

and...

2. What have you done to prepare for a career in law enforcement?

Now, I don't know you personally, so I have no idea as to why you want to work in the field of law enforcement, but because I've worked on the oral boards, I can give you some good talking points. Here are a few:

Why do you want a career in law enforcement?

- Rewarding work
- Exciting work
- I'm looking for a career not just a job
- Advancement opportunities
- Serving the community where I live
- Challenging job
- Good pay
- Good benefits
- I enjoy helping others
- A career I can be proud of
- A job I can look forward to going to every day

These of course are not an exhaustive list. Be creative and write down as many as you can in the space below. Give it some thought and really ask yourself why you want this job:

_____

_____

_____

_____

_____

_____

What have you done to prepare for a career in law enforcement?

The more answers you can give to this question, the better. It demonstrates your motivation, your enthusiasm and your personal desire to get the job. In many cases, this will help you stand out above your competition that may have done very little, to absolutely nothing to prepare for police work.

A good portion of police applicants have military backgrounds or they have completed courses in criminal justice. If you have neither of these, fear not. There is more to police work than this. Maybe you work in a service industry and you have a great deal of customer service experience. Police officers deal with people and your work in customer service, when presented right, goes a long way.

For example: "I work in a busy restaurant/grocery store/department store and I deal with the public extensively on a daily basis. I handle customer complaints and am often placed in stressful situations with unhappy customers. I believe that the patience and empathy I've developed in my current line of work will carry over and help me become a good police officer."

Hopefully you're working out and running on a regular basis. Not only is this good for your health, good physical conditioning is a must for the academy and in police work in general. Let your oral board know that you know that the job of a police officer is physically demanding and you've been preparing for it by lifting weights and running daily because you know their job can be physically demanding.

Have you talked to police officers about law enforcement? Recruiters are a good source of information and they're eager to talk to you. Call them up! Talk to them and ask questions…and let your oral board know that you've taken these steps. It tells them that you are serious.

If you have the time, enroll into a criminal justice course. This really tells the board that you are serious about becoming a police officer and that you are genuinely interested in the field of law enforcement. You can take classes online as well. The board doesn't care where you took the classes, but telling them you took classes will definitely score you points.

Most police departments allow citizens to ride along with their officers to get a "first hand" idea of what police work is really like. Call the department you are applying with and ask to do a ride-along. Let the board know that you've gone on a "ride along" (or two or three). This shows you took the initiative to really learn about police work.

If your oral board interview is tomorrow, and you haven't done any of the aforementioned, do something today! Get on the phone and talk to a recruiter, go to the bookstore and buy a book on police work, go to the police station and talk to the desk officer, get online and read forums about police work. Do something! Make sure you have an answer to this question. And keep in mind that the more you can answer, the better it will be for you.

Here are a few talking points:

Went on "ride-alongs" with the police department

Took college level courses in criminal justice

Attended department preparation seminars

Spoke to police recruiters

Spoke to police officers

Listen to police scanners

Went on police department tours

Worked as a Police Explorer or Cadet

Spoke to recent academy graduates

Spent time talking with friends/family members in law enforcement

List some things you have done to prepare for a career in law enforcement in the spaces below:

_____

_____

_____

_____

_____

_____

Volunteer:

If you have the time, volunteer at your local police department. This is an amazingly easy way to get to know members of the department and to learn "first hand" about the agencies policies, procedures, guidelines, culture, way of doing business, etc.

Ride-Alongs:

Most police departments allow the public to "ride along" with them through the course of their shift. This is a great way to learn about police work "first hand" from the officer's view. Call your local department and inquire about riding along.

College:

You can enroll in criminal justice courses online or at your local community college if you don't have the time to attend a large university. This is another great way to show your interest and to learn about the criminal justice system.

Study the Job Announcement:

I can't tell you how many people could have avoided failing their oral board interview if they had only studied the job announcement. Really, if you come to your interview and can't tell us what you think your duties and responsibilities will be as a police officer, then you have absolutely no business even showing up for your interview!

Knowing the job announcement inside & out can literally be your "secret weapon" to "acing" your oral board interview. The job announcement lets you know all the skills, abilities and knowledge needed to do the job. It also lists the minimum requirements (age, physical, etc) needed to perform the functions of the position. And, last but not least, the job announcement will list examples of the typical tasks and duties that you will be doing as a police officer, deputy, trooper, etc.

Simply put, the job announcement will give you many clues to the types of questions that may be asked during your oral board interview.

Below is a very detailed, very well written job announcement from the West Virginia State Police for the position of entry-level patrol officer:

JOB DESCRIPTION FOR STATE POLICE OFFICER
ESSENTIAL FUNCTIONS AND TASKS

It is a trooper's responsibility to perform basic police services in accordance with the mission, goals and objectives of the West Virginia State Police and in compliance with governing federal and state laws.

As outlined in Section 15-2-12 of the West Virginia Code, the West Virginia State Police shall have the mission of statewide enforcement of criminal and traffic laws with emphasis on providing basic enforcement and citizen protection from criminal depredation throughout the state and maintaining the safety of the state's public streets, roads and highways.

The essential functions and tasks required for the position of state police trooper, include, but are not limited to, qualification and use of firearms, providing emergency assistance conducting investigations, report writing and presenting testimony in a court of law.

STATE OF WEST VIRGINIA
JOB DESCRIPTION
BASIC PATROL OFFICER

JOB TITLE: ENTRY-LEVEL ROAD TROOPER

GENERAL STATEMENT OF DUTIES:
Under regular supervision, performs basic police services in accordance with the mission, goals and objectives of the West Virginia State Police and in compliance with governing federal and state laws.

Essential Functions and Tasks:

A. Essential Function - Arrest and Detain Persons

Essential Tasks:

1. Advise persons of constitutional rights (Miranda warning)
2. Arrest persons with a warrant
3. Arrest persons without a warrant (non-traffic)
4. Conduct temporary detention ("stop and frisk") of suspicious persons
5. Execute felony motor vehicle stop
6. Investigate suspicious vehicle
7. Plan how to make/execute arrests
8. Prepare information/complaint for filing of charges following arrest (criminal investigation)
9. Review warrants for completeness and accuracy
10. Obtain arrest warrants and/or make proper return
11. Check for wants/warrants on persons through DMV/NCIC

B. Essential Function - Protect Crime Scene and Collect Evidence and Information

Essential Tasks:

1. Collect evidence and personal property from crime scene
2. Diagram crime scenes
3. Document chain of custody for evidence
4. Dust and lift latent fingerprints
5. Examine evidence and personal property from crime scene to determine   importance
6. Package evidence or personal property
   Use camera (35mm/video camera, etc.)

7. Protect crime scene until specialized or back-up assistance arrives
8. Record location of physical evidence and fingerprints at scene
9. Secure crime scene
10. Initial/Mark/Label evidence
11. Determine area of crime scene
12. Search crime scenes for physical evidence
13. Search dead bodies for personal property/evidence
14. Recover and inventory stolen property
15. Tag evidence and confiscated property

C. Essential Function - Enforce DUI/Traffic Laws

Essential Tasks:

1. Observe person to recognize signs of drug or alcohol intoxication
2. Make custodial traffic arrest (e.g. DUI)
3. Administer roadside sobriety tests
4. Fill out warrant application to obtain drunk related blood/urine sample
5. Arrange for obtaining blood or urine sample for blood alcohol content (BAC)
6. Arrest DUI suspects
7. Determine probable cause to execute DUI stop
8. Operate "breathalyzer/intoxilyzer" type instrument to test blood alcohol content
9. Investigate hit and run violations
10. Investigate traffic accident scene to identify points of impact
11. Record statements of witnesses to traffic accidents
12. Assist trapped persons
13. Direct a moving vehicle out of a line of traffic to execute vehicle stop
14. Stop vehicles to arrest, cite or warn occupants

D. Essential Function - Operate Patrol Vehicle

Essential Tasks:

1. Engage in emergency driving in congested area
2. Engage in high speed pursuit or response driving off road
3. Engage in high speed pursuit or response driving on open road
4. Respond to crime in progress calls
5. Operate portable/car radio equipment

E. Essential Function - Conduct Search and Seizure

Essential Tasks:

1. Obtain search warrants and/or make proper return
2. Plan, organize and conduct raids
3. Observe person's body language to assess intentions/attitudes
4. Conduct field search of arrested persons
5. Conduct frisk or pat down
6. Search movable automobile under independent probable cause
7. Search persons with a court order (e.g. blood sample, hair sample)
8. Search premises or property incident to arrest
9. Search premises or property in hot pursuit/emergency situations
10. Search premises or property with consent
11. Search premises or property with warrant
12. Seize contraband
13. Search for a person in a darkened building or environment

F. Essential Function - Use Physical Force to Control Persons

Essential Tasks:

1. Confront, in a riot formation, groups of agitated people
2. Control hostile groups (e.g. demonstrators, rioters)
3. Use holds or devices to control or take suspect down
4. Tackle a fleeing suspect
5. Subdue physically attacking person
6. Use weaponless defense tactics
7. Subdue person resisting arrest
8. Use body pressure points to control person
9. Disarm violent armed suspect
10. Pull person out of vehicle who is resisting arrest
11. Strike a person with a side-handled baton
12. Strike a person with a straight baton
13. Use hammer lock to hold person
14. Use submission holds to control person
15. Locate and observe crowd agitators
16. Patrol riot stricken or civil disturbance areas
17. Physically restrain crowd
18. Catch a falling person to prevent injury
19. Use body language to project control and influence situation
20. Use voice commands to project control and direct actions
21. Hold flashlight in one hand while performing various police duties

G. Essential Function - Use Deadly Weapons

Essential Tasks:

1. Clean and inspect weapon
2. Discharge firearm at moving vehicle
3. Discharge firearm at night
4. Discharge firearm at person
5. Draw weapon to protect self or third party
6. Participate in firearms training
7. Secure firearm when off duty (e.g. home)
8. Fire weapon in dark environment with flashlight in one hand
9. Fire a weapon in nighttime combat (not including training)
10. Fire weapon in daytime combat (not including training)
11. Carry firearm when off duty
12. Discharge weapon at animal

H. Essential Function - Provide Emergency Assistance

Essential Tasks:

1. Determine existence of hazardous materials at scene of wreck, (e.g. train, vehicle, etc.)
2. Evacuate persons from dangerous areas (e.g. fire, chemical accident, etc.)
3. Secure accident and disaster scenes
4. Administer cardio-pulmonary resuscitation (CPR)
5. Administer mouth-to-mouth resuscitation
6. Apply basic first aid to control bleeding
7. Apply basic first aid to treat for amputations
8. Apply basic first aid to treat for choking (e.g. Heimlich method)
9. Talk with person attempting suicide to get them to stop or delay attempt
10. Use protective gear to prevent contact with infectious diseases

11. Take mentally deranged person into custody for their own protection
12. Mediate family disputes
13. Fire a weapon in dark environment with flashlight in one hand
14. Pull person out of a vehicle to perform a rescue
15. Place children in protective custody (e.g. child abuse)

I. Essential Function - Conduct Initial and Follow-Up Investigation of   Various Crimes and Events

Essential Tasks:

1. Conduct complete criminal investigations
Respond to and conduct preliminary investigation of events related to:
2. Homicide
3. Rape
4. Malicious Wounding
5. Attempted Murder
6. Burglary
7. Theft
8. Motor Vehicle Theft/Attempt
9. Arson and Bombing/Attempts
10. Weapons/Firearms Offenses
11. Sex Offenses
12. Controlled Substances
13. Family Offense
14. Domestic Violence
15. DUI - Intoxicants/Drugs
16. Fatal Traffic Accident
17. Vehicular Homicide
18. Vehicular Assault
19. Firearm Accidents

20. Death/Bodies Found
21. Disaster
22. Conduct on-the-scene suspect identifications (e.g. show-up or one-on-one suspect identification)
23. Conduct stationary surveillance of individuals or locations
24. Determine whether incidents are criminal or civil matters
25. Determine whether recovered property is linked with a previous crime
26. Exchange necessary information with other law enforcement officials (including intelligence information)

J. Essential Function - Write and Read Reports and Other Documents

Essential Tasks:

1. Complete initial offense report
2. Complete arrest reports
3. Complete criminal investigation report of felonies
4. Record confessions in writing

K. Essential Function - Present Testimony

Essential Tasks:

1. Present evidence in legal proceedings
2. Review reports and notes prior to court testimony
3. Testify at evidence suppression hearings
4. Testify at probable cause preliminary hearings
5. Testify before grand juries
6. Testify in criminal trials
7. Testify in court at implied consent hearings (e.g. DMV driver license revocation, breath test refusal)

L. Essential Function - Transport Persons in Custody

Essential Tasks:

1. Operate vehicle to transport prisoners
2. Search vehicle for weapons and/or contraband (e.g. before and after prisoner transport)

M. Essential Function - Conduct Interviews and Interrogations

Essential Tasks:

1. Interrogate adult suspects
2. Interview complainants, witnesses, etc.
3. Interview victims of sex crimes
4. Interrogate suspect or witness with use of polygraph results
5. Interview informants
6. Take statements of witnesses
7. Interrogate juvenile suspects

N. Essential Function - Conduct Traffic Accident Investigation

Essential Tasks:

1. Collect physical evidence from accident scene
2. Complete the standard DMV traffic accident report
3. Determine contributing factors to an accident
4. Diagram accident scenes
5. Protect traffic accident physical evidence for collection
6. Take precautions to prevent additional accidents at accident scene

Equipment Used in the Performance of Essential Tasks:

Roadside Alcohol Breath Test
Automobile
Baton
Body Armor
Fire Extinguisher
First Aid Kit
Road Flares
Flashlight
Flexicuffs
Handcuffs
Handheld Police Radio
Police Car Radio
P. A. System
Radar Unit
Semi-Automatic Pistol
Shot Gun
Lights and Sirens
Rubber Gloves
Ammunition/Magazine
Weapon Cleaning Equipment

More to Know...Before You Go:

There are a few more things to study-up on before your interview. Not doing so could result in major embarrassment that can easily "snowball" and ruin your interview.

1. The Law Enforcement Agency:

   Know the proper name and pronunciation of the agency. Know the name and proper title of the head of the department (police chief, sheriff, police commissioner, etc). Knowing the number of officers, and the diversity of officers will be to your advantage. Know about specialized units, community programs, etc. If the department has been in the news lately, it is good to familiarize yourself with that as well. Often the question is asked, "What can you tell us about the _____ police department?" You will impress the raters if you can give quite a few details about their department. Not knowing anything about the department, on the other hand, could be detrimental to your score.

2. The Community:

If you are applying to the police department that serves the community where you live, then chances are, you will already know a bit about the community. If you don't already know, find out what the community is like by doing some research. Look up the community's website for their economy, tourist attractions, population, and crime stats, city government, etc.

3. You:

Make sure that you know what is on your application. Review it prior to your interview because it is possible that you will be asked questions about your application. Remember who you put down for your references. The raters will have copies of your application in front of them under most circumstances. You don't want to be asked a question about your history and not know what they are talking about. Therefore, you also should not have lied or embellished anything on your application; this could immediately disqualify you from consideration.

Study:

I assume you purchased this book so that you can prepare yourself for the oral board interview. The questions provided in later chapters are designed for you to study and practice answering over and over again. Studying and really knowing your answers will show in the oral board interview.

Practice:

Prepare yourself mentally (besides physically and emotionally) and you will excel in your police oral board interview. Go over the questions again and again. Practice your answers out loud while you're driving to work...on your lunch break and on the way to your interview.

I cannot stress enough how important it is to practice answering questions on a tape recorder and/or in front of a video camera. This type of practice will not only allow you to get your answers down pat, it will greatly eliminate much of the anxiety most people have when they arrive for their oral board interview.

Remember, what you see on video and what you hear on tape IS how your oral board is going to see and hear you. There is no getting around this. When most of us hear ourselves on tape, we don't believe that is how we sound. But let me tell you something — that is how we sound!

Watching and listening to yourself answering the questions on the oral board will help you get rid of all your "umm's" and "uh's" and it can allow you to improve your voice's inflection and volume. Also, this type of practice, over and over again, will turn you into a much more polished speaker and believe me, the oral board panel will take notice.

If possible, another great method is to practice your answers in front of your friends and family. Trust me, there's a big difference between practicing your answers in your head and alone in front of the mirror then answering the questions out loud in front of people staring at you as the center of attention. Try to get comfortable with how you answer.

My suggestion is to buy a large pack of 3x5 index cards. Write the questions on the front and your answers on the back. Keep these cards with you everywhere you go. Then, at every chance you get, pull your cards out and start practicing.

I know many people will skip this step but I'm telling you, this is absolutely crucial to your success. Use these tips and practice all you can...on tape, in front of friends, on CD or MP3, wherever and whenever you can. You won't be sorry.

Know the Route:

It is imperative that you arrive on time (preferably 15 minutes early) to your oral board interview appointment. That being said, I strongly suggest that you learn and become familiar with where you need to be for your interview. Practice the route a week before you go at roughly the same time your interview is scheduled for. Find out how long it takes you to get there, taking into consideration the traffic, construction, delays, etc. On the day of the interview, allow yourself enough time for any unexpected delays. Trust me, if you are late, you will most likely be disqualified. Oral boards usually run late, but they will not wait for you!

Professional Appearance:

First impressions are important and because of that, I have devoted an entire chapter to dressing appropriately for the oral board interview. But, I also felt as though this topic should be covered in the preparation chapter because most people will want advanced preparation to get their hair cut, purchase a suit, and get together shoes and a professional looking shirt and tie to go with it.

Dressing for Success

For any interview, it is important to look the part. The first impression you give the board when you first walk in the room will go a long way and that impression will set the tone for how your oral board is going to think of you throughout the interview process. It may not be fair, but that is just the way it is. The clothes you wear tells the board that you respect them and you respect their position. It also tells them that you are a professional and that you are serious about the job you are applying for. This will be the first and only chance you'll get to impress those that are about to rate you for the position. You need to be at your 100% best!

Your oral board interview is a professional job interview in a comparatively conservative field. Because of that, it is expected that you dress accordingly. That being said, I strongly recommend a business suit and tie for males and a business suit for females. I do not recommend ever wearing shorts, jeans, flip flops, t-shirts, etc.

If you have any visible tattoos, I suggest you do everything in your power to cover them up. Try a skin colored bandage or make up. If you are a male who typically wears your hair long, consider a conservative haircut for this interview. If you have facial hair, consider getting rid of it for this interview.

Now, you don't need to wear a $2,000 Armani suit. What you need is a nice, clean, pressed suit that looks good on you. If you don't have a suit, go buy one. If you cannot afford a new suit, borrow or rent one.

There are always a few clueless applicants that come in slacks and a polo shirt and even jeans. They make a horrible first impression and it tells the raters (oral board) that you're really not serious about acquiring the job.

Follow these tips for looking your best at your interview:

Dress Standards for Men:

The Suit

If you're job hunting or serious about a career, you should own a suit. You don't have to buy the most expensive suit out there. There are many stores that sell nice business suits for affordable prices. And, chances are you will need this suit more than once. Suits should be worn to weddings, funerals, court, interviews, and high profile meetings.

A tie should always be worn with a long sleeve dress shirt. Do not pick a tie that will be distracting for the interviewers. You want them to remember you, not the picture of Daffy Duck on your tie. Pick a color such as red or blue with a very small, intricate design, or no design at all. Keep it simple...keep it professional.

If you plan to buy a suit before your interview, I would recommend black, navy blue or dark gray with a white shirt and a red tie. This is a standard, conservative look that you can wear anywhere. Avoid light colored suits. These have a more casual than professional look.

Your belt should match your shoes. Never wear a brown belt with black shoes and vice versa. With the color suits I recommend, you can do well with a black belt and black shoes. Your socks should match your pants in color. As far as a shirt, I strongly recommend white. This goes well with anything and it is a professional looking color.

Shine your shoes and do not wear shoes that are scuffed or have obvious marks and holes.

Dress Standards for Women

The Suit

For a law enforcement interview, this probably is not the time to wear the dress you wore to your boyfriend's best friend's wedding, or the sweet flowery dress you wear to church. Find yourself a professional suit-type outfit. Most retail outlets now sell business suits for women that include pants or a skirt, along with the shirt and jacket. If your suit includes a skirt, the skirt must not be any shorter than mid-knee when sitting. If you're unsure how short the skirt is, go with pants.

The shirt must be tucked in, and make sure the collar is neat and either outside the jacket or inside. It doesn't really matter as long as it is neat and pressed.

The shirt you wear under the suit jacket can either be long or short sleeved, but it should have a collar. You should also steer clear of having a shirt with a flamboyant print. It's much safer to go with a solid color.

Stay away from wearing the popular "lingerie" inspired camisoles underneath your suit jacket for your interview. Just like a man's flamboyant tie, your "lingerie-looking" camisole can be distracting to the interviewers and may shortchange you from giving your best professional performance.

The same rules about matching belts and shoes apply for women. See the men's section above. On the subject of shoes, however, stay away from sandals, flip-flops, and any open-toed shoes for the interview. The interviewers do not want to see your toenails. Wear shoes that you know you can walk in, comfortably. The stilettos are probably best left at home with that cocktail dress. Wear nylon socks (knee-high) if you are wearing a pantsuit and full nylons if you are wearing a skirt suit.

No matter what the trends are nowadays, you must wear nylons with your outfit to your interview, or else you risk looking unprofessional. While you hope your interview is like a day at the beach, you don't want to look like that's where you're going.

Other Standards for Men and Women:

Purses and Wallets

For women, your purse or briefcase should be a plain color and should not take away from your professional appearance. Brown or black, or the same color as your suit, would be safe. Refrain from "digging" through your purse while you are in the presence of the interviewers, as this relates disorganization to anyone watching you. Men, do not wear chains or spikes attached to your wallet. Put your wallet in your back pocket, out of sight.

Cellular Phones

Turn off your cellular phone or better yet, leave it in the car, when you arrive at the interview.

Pet hair

If you have pets, take a lint brush or roller with you in the car. When you get out at the interview site, brush your clothing down to remove all dog/cat hair. This may seem miniscule, but I don't like seeing someone who looks like they just rolled around with Fluffy, ten minutes before the interview.

Grooming

While you've got the attire down, you should now think about your grooming and personal appearance.

Men: Get a haircut. The most likely candidates that will be hired for a law enforcement officer already have the look. The hair is short and neat. Your head doesn't have to be shaved or completely bald (on purpose). You can have hair on the top of your head but make sure it is neat and you take care of it. Use a side part if it is a little longer on top or a little gel to hold it in place will do. The safest bet on hair length is to have your hair cut with a 3 or 4 (clippers) on top; no longer. Do not wear earrings, nose rings, eyebrow, or any other type of piercing.

Women: if your hair is long, put it up into a neat ponytail or bun, or secured back with a clip. If your hair is short, make sure it is neat and not overgrown. No hair should swing or hang below the jaw line. Also, your makeup (if worn) should be simple and clean. Stay away from dramatic colors and lines. Also, jewelry should be at a minimum as well; stud-type earrings in the ears (an earring in one hole in each ear) and one ring on a finger if you must. You don't want to be nervously playing with a bracelet or necklace during your interview.

Grooming Standards for Men and Women:

Shave! Shave, shave, shave, shave, shave. Do not have facial hair at your interview. I am not going to waste time talking about how it may or may not be trendy to have a little here but not a little there. The bottom line is, if you want to show the interviewers that you want the job, you're going to show up without any facial hair. Check your neck, ears, and nostrils as well. Ladies, if you're wearing a business type skirt, make sure your legs are shaved as well. Do not have leg hair poking out through your nylons. That is just unacceptable.

Nails: Women's nails should be neatly groomed. Remove chipped polish or get a manicure before your interview. Use a conservative or neutral color.

Men: It would be wise for you to cut your nails before the interview. Check to see if you have any dirt under them as well (although your shower should take care of that).

Your Smell: A shower is always a good idea daily, and before an interview where you're going to be wearing fresh, pressed clothes. Deodorant/anti-perspirant is also a good idea. Cologne or scented lotions, shave creams, and after shaves is not a good idea. I once interviewed a guy whom I could smell from all the way down the hall, before he even got to the interview. I don't know if he had taken a shower and then put on his cologne, or hadn't showered at all and was trying to cover his body odor, but I could not conduct the interview. The second time he came in, it was the same story and I told him, straight out, that I would not be able to interview him because of his cologne.

Ladies, the interview is not a time for colognes, perfumes, or scented lotions either. A fresh, clean shower and deodorant/anti-perspirant will do.

Teeth: Make sure you brush and floss your teeth. Use a mouthwash, mint, or chewing gum for fresh breath but when you get to the interview, spit out your gum. **DO NOT CHEW GUM IN YOUR INTERVIEW.** I can guarantee the interviewer will ask you to get rid of it and how awkward do you think that will be? Feel like you're back in 8th grade?

Hopefully, this chapter has provided some direction as to what to wear to your interview. Don't be the person who stands out negatively because they were not dressed professionally.

Etiquette with Everyone

You are going to deal with a lot of people throughout the interview process. Etiquette is of great importance. Each person you speak to should be treated with respect and courtesy. You never know who is watching you, evaluating you, or who you just may be working with someday. Use "sir," "ma'am," "please," and "thank you". Follow the directions you are given (which hall to walk down, which seat to sit in). If you need to call in to the department before your interview, be polite and courteous with each person you speak with on the telephone; a police department is an extremely busy place. Saying the wrong thing to the wrong person could jeopardize your place in the ranking process.

My secretary once warned me about a certain person who was going through the application process. She told me that when he called to schedule his interview, he was very disrespectful on the phone, claiming that the interview times she gave him were not good for his schedule. I hadn't even met the guy and already he had a strike against him because he was complaining to my secretary.

Making a Great First Impression

As the saying goes, "You only get one chance to make a first impression." We've already discussed how to dress and why. Remember, you're going to be sized up from top to bottom the second you are in front of the oral review board and you need to make this immediate impression a positive, lasting one.

At your first contact, be sure to shake hands (firmly) with every member of the review panel. Make good eye contact and introduce yourself if you weren't already introduced. Be polite. "Yes sir," "no ma'am," "please," and "thank you" are a must. Remember, everything you do is being evaluated. These oral board raters are gauging your professionalism. Using "sir" and "ma'am" is very professional.

During the interview, be enthusiastic and sell yourself. Normally, the interview begins with you being asked to tell the board about yourself. These are the questions you should be best prepared for and they should solidify a great first impression.

Your behavior is paramount to your success. Police graders will subconsciously compare your behavior to that what is expected of police officers by the public.

Have a structured answer in you mind that goes over your past employment, military, volunteer work and educational history. I know some people do not feel comfortable talking about themselves, but the oral board is truly a competition and if you leave out important details about the things you have accomplished in you life, then the raters will be unable to give you the score you deserve. Be enthusiastic and ready to sell yourself. If you're not comfortable selling yourself, you better get that way quick. Develop a "game face." Do what ever you have to do to let the oral board know that you are ready and willing to do what it takes to get the job. Confidence and enthusiasm will show during your interview and they will go a long way in making that great first impression.

Body Language Secrets

Your body language can reveal a lot to someone, without even saying a word. Police officers are experts in body language and they can easily pick up on common cues given by applicants. With that, you need to be aware of your body language and the image you portray.

Arms folded across the chest portrays that you're putting up a wall or barrier; you don't want to let others in; you don't care; you don't want to share; or it could mean that you're just nervous or simply not being honest. Even if you're nervous, folding your arms across the chest sends negative signals and you are sure to be marked down on your presence and/or communication skills.

Police officers on your oral board will notice your crossed arms so be cognizant not to cross them.

Keeping your hands in your pockets (and often fiddling with change or keys) signals that you are nervous or have something to hide.

Hands on the hips sends a signal of power or that you're in charge. Stay safe by leaving your hands comfortably at your sides or on your lap.

Make sure you make eye contact with each of the interviewers on the oral board during each of the questions you answer. Smile, and try to be relaxed while doing so. You don't want to stare someone down, or make them feel uncomfortable. Too much eye contact can be as bad as no eye contact. If you're uncomfortable with looking the interviewers straight in the eyes, shoot for just above their eyeballs, at the eyebrow.

The oral board expects you to be nervous. We've all been there. Sitting across from three intimidating police officers in uniform is not easy and the oral board is aware of that. Even though you are nervous, try to act as relaxed as possible. Remember to breathe. If you have to stand while waiting, remember not to lock your knees- you don't want to pass out at the police oral review board!

Commonly Asked Oral Board Questions for Law Enforcement

The following are commonly asked questions that are regularly being asked in oral board interviews by various law enforcement agencies across the country. This is not a guarantee that all (or even any) of these questions will be asked, but they have been recently collected and reviewed and I'm confident that you will see several of them (in one form or another) in your own oral board interview.

Also, keep an open mind. The questions here may not be worded exactly as they will be in your own oral board interview. So, it is important to have a firm grasp on what the question is getting at, instead of focusing primarily on memorizing the answers themselves.

The goal of this manual is to prepare you and help you study. Every interview will be different and your preparation will be the key to success.

Again, pay close attention to what the question is getting at. The questions asked of you are not normally geared to trick you, so do not assume that the dynamics of a question are different from what is asked.

Some Things to keep in Mind:

Police officers are held to a higher standard than the general public. Despite what you see in the movies, we do not cover up for others and we don't stand by and watch police officers commit crimes and break the rules. Just as we enforce the laws of citizens, we must also enforce the rules and regulations of the department.

We do not give police officers preferential treatment— they are not allowed to be intoxicated on the job, they are not allowed to steal, they aren't allowed to batter their spouses, they are not allowed to sleep on the job, etc.

We are not afraid to call for backup—we want to go home every night to our families and we want to make sure our partners do the same. We are not superhuman with invincible powers. Keeping these points in mind will help make answering those questions a lot easier.

Keep in mind that the oral board panel is trying to determine whether or not you are going to be able to handle a job in law enforcement. They want to know if you can work as a team and to get things done, no matter how hard they appear.

The interview is the only chance you'll have to let the board know who you are and what you will bring to the position. They will ask you questions that will cover some, if not all, of the following topics (many of which we have already addressed):

- Communications skills

- Job knowledge

- Preparation

- Integrity

- Honesty

- Dependability/Stability

- Maturity

- Ability to function within a strict set of rules & regulations

- Ability to work without constant supervision

- Self Control

- Good Judgment

- Empathy/Caring for Others

- Common Sense

- Self-confidence

- Assertiveness

- Motivation

- Dedication

- Enthusiasm

- Flexibility/Adaptability

- "Team Player"

Q.   **Why do you want to be a police officer?**

Q.   **What have you have you done to prepare for a career in law enforcement?**

We went over these two questions in an earlier chapter. Be sure to review these as they are probably the most standard of all questions asked in law enforcement oral board interviews.

You should start putting an extensive list together, answering these two questions right away. They are usually some of the first questions asked and they can definitely set the tone for the remainder of your interview. Answering the first few questions with good, solid answers will definitely strike up the confidence you need to successfully get through the rest of the interview.

Q. Can you tell us why you feel you are the best-qualified applicant for this job?

Q. Tell us about yourself.

Tell them anything that is positive and try to relate it to police work.

"I have lived in this community for x number of years. I have been studying criminal justice at the local university while working as a customer service specialist at a local retailer. I like hunting on my off time and spending time with my friends/family/pets, etc"

Q. Describe your background and experience as it relates to the job as a law enforcement officer.

"I have served in the military so I am familiar with some practices of law enforcement."

"I earned a degree from ____ university in criminal justice."

"I have been working as a night guard at a security company."

"I work out on a regular basis because I know the job can be physically demanding."

"Although my current job is not in law enforcement, it gives me a great deal of contact with the public."

"I've attended police preparation seminars, read police related books, participated in police related discussion forums."

Q. Why do you want to become a law enforcement officer?

"I am looking for a career that will enable me to help others. I find law enforcement exciting and I think it would be a fulfilling career."

Q.   Why do you want to become a law enforcement officer with this department in this city?

Tell them why you like the department. Some topics could include how it is a progressive department, technologically advanced, or that you have researched other agencies and you feel that this one is best regarding training, reputation, and room for promotion. Here are some other answers:

"I have lived in this city for ___ (x number of years) and I feel that I have a duty to protect and serve the people in my community, as well as my family and friends."

"I prefer to work for this department over larger departments because of its size. I want to feel like I'm doing good and making a difference, rather than just being a number in a flood of officers in a large department."

Or…

"I prefer a larger police department over a smaller one because of the tremendous opportunities available. Eventually, after I have become a successful patrol officer, I may want to work in a specialized unit like the detective bureau, K9, SWAT, and I know that your department offers such opportunities."

Q.   Describe the kind of work you expect to be doing as a new officer.

"I know that I could be assigned to work any shift. I expect to patrol my assigned area, work with limited supervisions, answer calls for service (from simple report calls to serious crimes in progress), settle disputes, conduct traffic stops, write citations, and make arrests."

Remember to review/study the job announcement

Q.   Describe a difficult problem that you have had to overcome in your life.

"I used to be painfully shy. I could not speak in front of a crowd or group of people. I was socially introverted and preferred to be by myself. I started to feel like I had to change or else I would miss out on a lot of opportunities in life. I took a communications class at my college, which got me up and talking in front of people. I also joined "Toastmasters" which has helped me a great deal."

Q.   When do you think it is appropriate for a police officer to use physical force?

"I think it is appropriate for a police officer to use physical force when the suspect or person they are dealing with is not complying with the officer's commands, or if the officer is met with physical force from that person."

Q.   What interests you most about a career in Law Enforcement?

"I am most interested in the challenge the career presents and how rewarding I think police work will be."

Q.   What is your biggest accomplishment?

List any accomplishment that would show your strength as a police officer.

Q.   How would your friends describe you? How would your family describe you?

"My friends would describe me as a fun person and that I have a good sense of humor, but also someone who is honest and hard-working. My family would say the same thing. They would probably also say that I am driven and have a desire to accomplish my goals and that I am dependable."

Q.   What are your major strengths?

"I know how to set goals and what to do to achieve them. I am also very good when it comes to memorization. I am able to memorize lots of data and facts, which I believe will help me in this job. I know that police officers have to remember lots of laws, regulations, codes, and call signs, as well as names and faces."

Q.   What are your major weaknesses?

You will not want to put any sort of negative light on yourself so try and answer these types of questions positively, like: "I am very organized and sometimes it can be a fault of mine." Do not give them a weakness that would be disqualifying, such as "I'm a kleptomaniac — I just can't help stealing things."

Q.   This job requires working shift work, holidays, weekends, and court appearances on days off. How do you think this will affect your personal life?

"I realize that this type of career will require some lifestyle changes, however, it is a career that I want to have and am willing to make those sacrifices. My family knows how important this is to me and we have discussed some of the differences in our lifestyle that this career will bring. We are ready for the challenge and my family is supportive."

Q. How have you prepared to deal with the unpleasant parts of police work, such as working in extreme heat and/or cold, witnessing death and serious injuries, dealing with hostile and violent subjects?

"I've put a lot of thought into this career prior to applying. I know that it's a tough job and it's not for everyone. While I haven't had to deal with such unpleasant situations before, I've been in previous positions where I've had to rise to the occasion to accomplish tasks and meet the expectations of others. This job will be no different. I feel that I'm mentally and physically prepared for the job and that after training, I'll be even more ready to handle the unpleasant parts of the job."

Q. What have you done to prepare for this job?

"I have researched the job and feel that it is the one for me. I created a physical fitness routine and have found myself to be ready for the police academy. I have studied the laws of this municipality and the state. I attended a preparation seminar. I have gone on ride-alongs. I have spoken with recruiters and other police officers to find out what it takes to be successful in the academy."

Q. To you, what is the role of a law enforcement officer?

"Someone who serves others. He has a duty to protect others and help those in need. He is a model of citizenship. He obeys and follows the laws, because he enforces them."

Q. How do people in the community perceive law enforcement officers?

Give a positive answer, such as, "People in the community view law enforcement as a protection and a resource for them."

Q.   How do you handle stress?

Explain things you do to handle tension so that it does not build up inside you (i.e.: exercise, play sports, listen to music, think about my kids, play with my dog).

Q.   Explain how you would be able to work under pressure.

"I think that I would be able to work well under pressure. Not that I am a procrastinator, but I feel that I work better when I know I have to get something done in a specific amount of time. I can think on my feet and I perform best when there is a limited amount of time to make decisions."

Q.   If you could work any assignment, what would it be?

"I am willing to accept anything that the department assigns me, but I think I would have the most fun working as a detective. I love to solve problems and believe that I would do well at being assigned an open case and solving it."

Q.   What do you think would be your least favorite assignment?

"I am willing to accept anything that the department assigns to me but I think it would be hard to work elder abuse cases. My own grandparents are very special to me and I would find it hard to investigate those who abuse the elderly."

Q.   If hired, how long do you plan to stay with our department?

Understand that law enforcement agencies spend a lot of money to hire and train you and they want to know that this is your chosen career instead of just another job.

"I plan to make this my career and if I was hired, I would plan on staying with the department until I retire."

Q.   Describe how you are able to work efficiently by yourself.

"I like to be busy and am always looking for something to do. If I was alone and had down time I would busy myself by either patrolling and looking for things that aren't right or I would ask my supervisor what I could do to help him out."

Q.   Describe how you are able to work efficiently with a team.

"I understand that a team uses each person's strengths to complete a task. I would contribute my strengths to the team effort so that we all get something out of meeting the goal at hand."

Q.   What is multi-tasking?

"Multi-tasking is the ability to perform several duties at once."

Q.   Do you have multi-tasking abilities and if so describe how you multi-task.

"I've just always been a "busy" person. I can carry on a conversation while watching T.V. and working at the computer, all at the same time."

Q. **Do you feel that physical fitness plays a role in effective policing? Explain why or why not.**

"Yes, I feel that you have to be physically fit to deal with people who are of all strengths and sizes, who may be under the influence of drugs or alcohol, or who have their adrenaline pumping because of a situation. I also think that the public forms certain perceptions about police officers who aren't physically fit looking- that they are government employees who don't do anything."

Q. **Give an example where you would feel it would be ok to give up your gun.**

Just know this - it is never ok to give your gun to anyone.

A: "I would never give up my gun to anyone in any situation."

Q. **Are you prejudiced against any race, nationality, or religion?**

"No. I have friendships with many different people and do not separate anyone because of their race or religion. My own family is made up of people from different backgrounds and religions. Every human being should be treated equally and fairly."

Q. **What is community policing?**

"Community Policing is a policing strategy where the police and the community work together to fight crime."

Q. **Do you think community policing is an important role within the police department?**

"Yes, community policing allows the police officers to stay in specific neighborhoods so that they can be more familiar with the residents they serve while creating a bond of trust with that community. Also, the community gets to play a more active role in reducing crime in their neighborhoods."

Q.   How would you describe deadly force?

Deadly force is any force that could result in serious injury or death. "I know that deadly force is a reality of police work and that it could happen my first day on the job or never in my career. Although I hope to never be in a deadly force situation, I am prepared to use deadly force if it becomes necessary."

Q.   What have you learned in previous jobs that you think will help you in your career as a police officer?

"Probably the most important thing I've learned is responsibility. I understand that when a supervisor tells me to do something, that he expects me to get it done and that I am then responsible for completing what was expected of me."

Q.   Why do you want to leave your current job?

"I do like my current job, but I have planned for a career in law enforcement. I chose law enforcement over my current job because of the challenges it provides."

Q.   Why should we pick you over the other applicants?

"I don't know the qualifications of the other applicants, but I can tell you that I have done a lot to prepare for this position and that I will give 110% to be successful at it. This is the only career that I am interested in and I will do whatever it takes to get this position."

Q.   Do you hold any prejudices?

"I don't hold any prejudices against any race or sex, however, I can tell you in all honestly that I do have some bias with regards to child molesters, rapists, murders, etc. However, I understand that as a law enforcement professional, I will be dealing with these types of people and I will do so in accordance with the law."

Situational Questions

After the first round of short questions, you will be given a few scenarios and asked to respond on how you would handle each situation. This gives the board an opportunity to assess your judgment and reasoning ability. Take your time and reason through the questions. Remember, the oral board is not looking for you to be an experienced police officer. What they are looking for, however, is to see that you have sound reasoning and good judgment and that you are a person of honesty and integrity.

A situational question will start with a story, usually placing you as a police officer encountering a situation that requires immediate action. Listen closely to the story. They will normally be disguised and require you to "uncover" what is really going on. Once the question is asked, you should ask yourself, "What is really going on here?"

An example of one particular question that I see people lose it on so often is this:

The oral board panel tells you that you are required by law to make an arrest in a domestic battery case if you can determine the primary physical aggressor in the case. When you arrive on scene, you determine that a domestic battery has occurred and that the male party is the primary physical aggressor. However, the female party insists that she doesn't wish to press charges. What do you do?

Again, you have to sit back and think. Even though the female party does not wish to press charges, you were told up front that you are LEGALLY REQUIRED to make an arrest. So, my point again is that you have to take off the mask and do what is right. Masks are the sneaky ways that the oral board will try to throw you off. Pay close attention, sit back and think about what is really happening, and then give them your answer.

Q: You arrive at a report of a burglary at a convenience store. The store is closed for the night. After you and your backup officer check out the store, it appears that the person has stolen the register drawer and is nowhere to be found. Dispatch tells you that the storeowner is on his way to assess the damage. While waiting, your fellow officer opens a package of chips and eats them, and throws the bag away. He then takes a few candy bars off of the shelf and puts them in his patrol car. He says that the owner will never miss them. What do you do?

A: "I would be comfortable knowing that I didn't do anything wrong. However, I would not be comfortable with my fellow officer's actions and I would tell him so. I would try to get him to put the candy back. If he didn't, I would report it to my supervisor after we were finished with the situation."

Q: During a traffic stop, the driver of the car seems inebriated and smells of alcohol. When you initiate a field sobriety test, the driver fails. As you are preparing to take the offender to jail, he tells you that he is the son of the City Manager. He goes on to tell you that if you take him to jail, he will make sure that his father has you fired. What do you do?

A: "He broke the law and as an officer I could not release someone who would be endangering himself and others by driving while intoxicated. I would make sure that my report was detailed and captured every event of the traffic stop, including the threat about my job. Further, because he is the relative of a high-ranking official, I would notify my supervisor while at the scene."

Q: You have conducted a traffic stop and you're in the middle of issuing a traffic citation when a violent crime in progress in your assigned area comes over the radio. What course of action would you take?

A: "I would immediately stop writing the citation and tell the driver of the vehicle that he can go with a warning and I would rush to the violent crime in progress. Since it is a violent crime, there's a good chance someone could be hurt, or worse, and protecting someone's life is far more important and takes priority over a traffic citation."

Q: You and your partner arrest a subject for a theft at a local department store. After the subject is handcuffed and taken into custody, he is placed in the back of your patrol car. As you are getting ready to leave, the suspect begins calling your partner names. Your partner opens the door and punches the suspect in the face and walks away. What do you do?

A. "If the suspect is already handcuffed and under control, punching the suspect is uncalled for. The first thing I would do is to get the suspect medical attention if needed. I would address my partner to see what was said and what had happened. I would then notify my supervisor and request him to respond to the scene. Once he arrived, I would explain what happened. I understand my partner is angry, but he is not legally allowed to commit a crime against someone in custory."

Q: You are assigned to conduct traffic enforcement in a local school zone because of numerous complaints of

speeders in the area. You observe a car traveling at a high rate of speed and effect a traffic stop. When you get up to the driver's window, you find that the driver is your mother-in-law. What course of action would you take?

Remember, besides judging your decision making, you are being judged on your honesty. Would you really give your family member a traffic ticket?

A: "I know that police have discretion in issuing tickets vs. giving a warning. In this case, I would issue a warning. However, I'd inform my mother-in-law that she's putting me in a bad position and I'd warn her to slow down and advise her of the dangers of speeding in a school zone."

Q. You are on patrol in a business district at 2:00 AM when you find the front door of a business that appears to be pried open. What do you do first?

A. Your first action should be to notify dispatch and to get a backup unit to your location. For safety reasons, you do not enter scenes like these by yourself.

Q: You and a fellow officer are eating lunch at a local restaurant. When your meal is finished, the waitress brings you the bill and you find that you were not charged and the waitress tells you that your meal is free. What would you do?

This question is an integrity question.

A: "I would thank the waitress and explain that the gratuity was not necessary. If the waitress insists, I would leave enough money to cover my half of the bill. While I don't want to tell the restaurant how to conduct their business, accepting gratuities can shed a poor light on the department and the profession and could cause bigger problems down the road. If my partner refused to pay his half of the bill, I would speak to him about it in private and inform him of how it looks on the department when/if we take gratuities. If he still refused, I would inform my supervisor."

Q: You and another officer respond to a burglary call at a home. As you go through the house and find no one there, you observe your partner take a $20 bill off a dresser and put it in his pocket. No one else witnesses this but you. How would you address this situation?

This is another integrity question.

A: "This officer has committed a theft. I would speak to him about it immediately. I would tell him that I saw him take it and I would also immediately report it to my supervisor. If an officer will steal $20 while someone is there watching, what could he be stealing when no one is around?"

Q: One of the officers on your squad, who is a very good friend of yours, shows up for work and you smell beer on his breath. You believe that he has been drinking. You also believe that this officer who is your friend has a drinking problem. What are you going to do?

A: "I would immediately inform my supervisor. Even though he is a good friend, his actions could put many people in jeopardy, not to mention the police department's reputation. This officer carries a gun and will likely be driving a patrol car. Being under the influence of alcohol puts far too many people at risk to ignore this behavior."

Q: In this state, it is mandatory that you make an arrest when a domestic battery occurs. You respond to a domestic violence call and upon arrival you discover

that the male in the situation is a police officer with another local law enforcement agency. The female is claiming he beat her and has several marks on her face consistent with being beaten. Your investigation is consistent with her story. He takes you aside and tells you that he cannot go to jail or he will lose his career as a police officer. After you finish speaking with him, she approaches you again and says that she does not want to press charges, and begs you not to arrest him. Explain what you would do.

A: "Because it is mandatory to make an arrest, I have no discretion in the matter even though the male is a police officer and the female does not want to press charges. Therefore, I would arrest the male."

Q: You are dispatched to a fight in progress at a local bar. When you arrive, you see that the fight is still in progress. What actions would you take to stop the fight?

Always remember that at any scene, it is imperative to take control of the situation by separating the parties involved. At that time, you will interview witnesses separately to get to the heart of the matter so that you can take the next step (arrests, citations, trespass, etc).

Q: You are off-duty at a party when you notice several of the partygoers begin to smoke marijuana. What would you do?

You should leave this situation immediately and report it to the police. You do not want to be around illegal activity and you do not wanting someone to report that you remained at this party when you knew illegal activity was occurring regardless of whether or not you participated.

Q: You are patrolling your assigned area when you see what appears to be a shop owner in front of his store with a gun in his hand.

The board is attempting to see if you will just assume that this is a storeowner and to see if you will approach him in a lackadaisical manner. Let the board know that you will approach the situation in a safe manner and that you will notify dispatch and request backup before trying to make contact with the subject. Anytime a gun is involved, it can be a deadly situation.

Q: You get called to a home because someone believed child abuse was going on. You hear a child crying in the home but when you ask to come in the man will not allow you and tells you to get a warrant. What do you do?

You have a community caretaking role that allows you to enter to ensure the safety of that child without a warrant. The immediate safety of human beings is necessary in this situation as this could be a life and death matter.

Q: You are dispatched to a traffic accident. Put these three things in the order you would do them and give a reason for doing so: control traffic, check for injuries, interview witnesses.

Always check for injuries first and get paramedics in route if necessary. Secondly, you would control traffic so no one else gets hurt. Third would be talking to witnesses after everyone is safe.

Q: You respond to backup another unit in an alley. When you arrive you see a man running away and the officer at the scene is yelling at you, "Shoot him, shoot him" What will you do?

You do not shoot anyone unless you know that a person is about to severely injure or cause the death of someone. Shooting someone requires imminent jeopardy. If you do not see someone's life being in imminent jeopardy then you do not shoot—no matter what another officer tells you.

Q: You are flagged down by a woman in a parking lot. The woman tells you that she found her son playing with a gun and she would like you to have a talk with her son about the dangers of playing with guns. What do you do?

A. You take the time to have a talk with the child about the dangers of playing with guns.

> **I include this question to make sure that you understand the police officer role of community service—that police work is not all chasing "bad guys." If you do have a question such of this—and one that would be in the realm of the police officer's knowledge—you should take action to be involved with the community you serve.**

Q: You and your partner are driving a dangerous prisoner to the jail. While en route to the jail, you observe an accident involving three vehicles. It appears that damage to the vehicles is significant. What would you do?

A. You stop to render aid and radio for additional units and medical personnel (if needed) while your partner stands by with the prisoner still locked in the vehicle.

Q: While off duty, you go to a convenience store to purchase a few items. No one in the store knows you are a police officer. While you are paying for the items, the cashier engages in a conversation with you. She mentions that she believes she received a counterfeit twenty-dollar bill today. What would you do?

A. Tell her she should report the crime to the police right away. Advise her that if possible, she should secure any surveillance tape evidence and write down a description of the suspect who passed the bill.

Q: For the past several months, there have been many assignments which required someone to work late at night. Everyone in your office has done their share of working late hours except for one person. His continual refusal to work after hours is causing a strain with his co-workers. What would you do?

A. "I would confront this officer because he is bringing the morale of the shift down by not carrying his weight. If there is a problem at home or in his personal life, I would urge him to get help. If it turns out that he is being selfish and unconcerned about the other members of the shift, then I would bring the matter to my supervisor."

More Questions to Consider

How do you think your experiences in work or at home can help you deal with an angry crowd? What steps would you take to handle the situation?

_____

_____

_____

_____

_____

_____

Explain to us an unpopular decision you had to make and what the outcome of that decision was?

_____

_____

_____

_____

_____

_____

Tell us about a difficult problem you had to overcome and what you did to overcome the problem?

_____

_____

_____

_____

_____

_____

_____

What are your strengths and weaknesses and how would they affect your performance as a police officer?

_____

_____

_____

_____

_____

_____

_____

If you are placed in area where you are the minority, will you have any trouble doing your job?

_____

_____

_____

_____

_____

_____

How do you feel about having a woman as your boss or a woman having authority over you?

_____

_____

_____

_____

_____

_____

If you were put in a situation where you had to take someone's life, would you be able to do so?

_____

_____

_____

_____

_____

_____

_____

How does your family feel about the career you have chosen and are they aware of the risk of you being killed on duty? Have you discussed this with them and how do they feel?

_____

_____

_____

_____

_____

_____

_____

How do your past experiences relate to you becoming a police officer?

_____

_____

_____

_____

_____

_____

_____

Describe how and why you would use your social skills to defuse a situation?

_____

_____

_____

_____

_____

_____

If you were confronted with a situation where your action was legally justified but against your moral values, what would you do?

_____

_____

_____

_____

_____

_____

What is the most stressful situation you've been in and how did you handle it?

_____

_____

_____

_____

_____

_____

Your Field Training Officer (FTO) and you make an arrest of a homeless man who spits on.the FTO. The FTO punches the man in the stomach, what do you do?

_____

_____

_____

_____

_____

_____

_____

Your Sgt. breaks a Department rule and tells you to keep quiet about it. What do you do?

_____

_____

_____

_____

_____

_____

_____

What can you bring to the department and community?

_____

_____

_____

_____

_____

_____

_____

Could you arrest someone for a law you don't like?

_____

_____

_____

_____

_____

_____

_____

Why should we hire you?

_____

_____

_____

_____

_____

_____

What would you do if someone spit on you while they were in handcuffs?

_____

_____

_____

_____

_____

_____

What would you do if someone spit at you (not hitting you)?

_____

_____

_____

_____

_____

_____

_____

What would you do if someone who was not under arrest but you have reasonable suspicion to detain refuses to give you their name or not even speak at all?

_____

_____

_____

_____

_____

_____

Tell us about your experience and training as it relates to the position of Police Officer?

_____

_____

_____

_____

_____

_____

Why are you considering a career in law enforcement?

_____

_____

_____

_____

_____

_____

_____

What are your qualifications?

_____

_____

_____

_____

_____

_____

How would you rate your ability to get along with others? What is the basis for this rating?

_____

_____

_____

_____

_____

_____

How effective are you in working in a team environment and why?

_____

_____

_____

_____

_____

_____

_____

What motivates you to put forth your greatest effort?

_____

_____

_____

_____

_____

_____

_____

How would you describe your work ethic?

_____

_____

_____

_____

_____

_____

How has your education and training prepared you for a career in law enforcement?

_____

_____

_____

_____

_____

_____

What accomplishment has given you the most satisfaction and why?

_____

_____

_____

_____

_____

_____

_____

In what kind of work environment are you most comfortable?

_____

_____

_____

_____

_____

_____

_____

Deadly Force Scenarios

More likely than not, there will be a situational question regarding the use of deadly force. The following questions are good examples. The scenario could vary vastly, but you need to know that your failure to let the oral board know that you can and will use deadly force if necessary is crucial to passing your oral board interview. There are far too many police officer applicants that fail the oral board because of this one question. It is, in fact, the most important question on the oral board. The biggest mistake is that applicants try to handle the deadly force situation using everything but deadly force. They say they would give a warning, then another warning, then call for back up, then find cover, then try to talk the guy into dropping a gun, they even say they'll try to shoot the gun out of someone's hands, etc.

You need to face facts. Police officers encounter deadly force situations all the time. And, it is quite common for police officers to have to use deadly force and take lives to protect others.

Don't think too much about this question. It might be subtle. But, if the question has one person in a position to take the life of another person (a knife, gun, etc), tell the oral board that you will shoot the suspect to stop him from hurting someone else.

If you let the oral board think that you aren't prepared to use deadly force, you will not pass the oral board interview. This is a "do or die" question (no pun intended). If you can't honestly say that you're prepared to take a life in the course of your duties, I can honestly say that you are, in fact, not ready for police work.

Q: You pull over a car for a minor traffic violation. As you approach the car, the driver holds what appears to be a gun out the window and is pointing it at you. What do you do?

You need to take fast, decisive action or you could be killed. Someone is pointing a gun at you and you are a trigger pull away from being shot. In this case, you would need to draw your weapon and shoot. You do not have time to "dance" around looking for cover, calling for backup and ordering the subject to drop the weapon. Be sure to let the board know this is your thought process as you will be scored on your reasoning. Tell them that since you are a trigger pull away from being killed, you would take this quick, decisive action.

Q. You and several other officers are attempting to arrest a subject at his residence. As you are walking up to the house the front door opens and the subject appears. He steps out of the doorway and onto the front porch. He has a gun in his hand and he begins shooting at you. What would you do?

A. "I would return fire while making my way to cover without taking my eyes off the suspect."

Q. You have been dispatched to a domestic violence call at a residence that you've been called out to before. Upon arrival you see another officer interviewing a female subject in front of the apartment. As you are exiting your vehicle you see a man approaching the other officer with a handgun behind his back. How would you react to this situation?

A: "I would challenge the male and tell him to drop the gun with my gun pointed at him so that I can fire immediately, if necessary. This would alert the officer to the danger. Hopefully, the subject with the gun will drop it at that point. However, if he refused to drop the gun immediately, I would be forced to shoot the male to prevent him from taking the life of the other officer and the female."

In this scenario, the subject had the gun behind his back, which gives you a reason to challenge him at first. If the gun was pointed at someone or if he does not drop it immediately, you have no choice but to shoot.

Keep in mind that as a police officer, you are sworn to protect the lives and property of others. When someone could be seriously injured or killed by the deliberate actions of another, you will be within your rights to use deadly force to protect that person. Let the board know that you are willing to take a life if necessary.

Willingness Questions

Willingness questions are also paramount to passing the oral board interview. These questions are easy to answer and they're usually asked near the end of the interview. Their purpose is to assess your willingness to do what is expected of you in police work. A single "no" answer to any of these questions will likely put an immediate end to your interview.

Examples:

Q: Are you willing to use deadly force to take a life, if necessary, in the performance of your duties as a police officer?

A: "YES."

Q: Are you willing to comply with departmental rules, regulations, policies and procedures?

A: "YES."

Q: Are you willing to wear a uniform, carry a gun and comply with department grooming standards?

A: "YES."

Q: Are you willing to work any shift (day or night) as well as weekends and holidays?

A: "YES."

Ending the Interview — Selling Yourself

After the questions are complete, the oral board panel will usually ask if there is anything you would like to add. Keep in mind that your score has not been totaled yet and this is a prime opportunity to sell yourself a little more. While this question is not scored, it can have a major impact on your overall score on the oral board.

Let me explain that.

There are definitely wrong answers on the oral board interview — answers that can eliminate you from contention on the spot. However, how you answer the other questions on the test are somewhat subjective. And, they are graded by humans, so there will always be some subjectivity in scoring (hence an oral board instead of just one interviewer).

With that, it is important to use this as an opportunity to sell yourself as best you can. In fact, if it were me, I'd act like a gun was to my head and that if I didn't sell myself enough, someone was going to pull the trigger.

All too often, I see candidates "on the bubble" (between passing and failing), waste this precious opportunity.

And all too often, the interviewee is so "beat down" and exhausted from the stress of the interview, they just want to get out of there. When they are asked, "Is there anything you'd like to add?" they reply with a simple, "No," answer because they want nothing more than the interview to be over.

This does nothing for you!

When given the opportunity to add to the interview, first thank the board for their time and the opportunity to speak with them…then go to work!

You should go on and on about yourself at this point. Throw everything you have at them. Bring up everything you were prepared to answer but were not asked. Tell them about your excitement about the job (police love this), reiterate your preparation, work ethic, etc.

If it were me, I'd probably go on and on until they physically removed me from the room (you shouldn't take it this far—but you get my point).

So, I would take the time right now to sell yourself on paper. Write down and memorize what you're going to say and be ready to sell yourself during the oral board interview.

Tell them that you are doing fine financially right now…but that you are working an unsatisfying job and you want a fulfilling career. Let the board know that your applying with their department is not being done on a whim, but that you have thought long and hard about becoming a police officer and that you have the backing and support of your family. Tell them that you have looked at other agencies and let them know why you want to work with them over other agencies.

Some of the questions I've provided may not be asked. You should, however, know them all because you can use your knowledge of these answers to sell yourself at the end.

For example, if you were never asked about community policing, when selling yourself at the end of the interview, you could tell them that you're familiar with community policing and you're excited about the opportunity to work closely with the community in solving problems and keeping the community safe.

If you are not asked about your prior employment and how it relates to police work, you could add it now. You could say, "My current job gives me a great deal of contact with the public and because of that, I've really become a "people person" and I've learned how to deal effectively with people and their problems."

As you exit the interview, be sure to shake hands with each board member. If you can, call them by name, "Thank you Sgt. Smith."

Quick Interview Tips

- Do not interview if you are not prepared.

- Sit up straight.

- Maintain eye contact.

- Listen to the question: When asked a specific question, you need to give a specific answer. Pay close attention to what is being asked and stay on point.

- Take your time: Before answering any question, take your time to organize your thoughts and frame your answer.

- Do not try to B.S. the panel with long-winded answers that skirt questions you don't know. Just tell the board that you don't know.

- Use an appropriate volume of speech: not too loud and not too soft.

- Use only words you can pronounce and completely understand.

- Don't make jokes.

- Don't interrupt board members.

- Be confident.

- Do not display any nervous mannerisms.

- Thank the board at the end of the interview.

Final Thoughts

Remember, the law enforcement agency that you are applying with is not looking for people who are just "testing the water." They want people who are career minded and who plan on a career with that agency and for it to be the last job they will ever have. You need to let them know that this is how you feel about the job.

Your investment into this book tells a great deal about you. You want to become a police officer and you'll do whatever it takes to get the job. You're not one to give up or quit. You know what you want and you put your all into it. I commend you for that...because you're already demonstrating a police mindset.

You will be expected to be nervous during your oral board interview but you will be expected to get your nervousness under control at some point. Take deep breaths...and don't talk too fast. Take your time...think your answers through and then give them with confidence!

The interview is just the beginning of many tests that will come with a law enforcement career; you are tested in the academy; you are tested for certifications; you are evaluated by your supervisor; and you are tested every day on the job.

Congratulations on your decision to become a law enforcement officer. And good luck on your oral board interview and all that is to come.

Keep this guide with you and use it for all the oral interviews you do, as it will be a priceless resource.

I have included a Police Officer's Oath in this guide for good reason. This oath will give you a good background from where your answers should come from. It provides a framework for what is expected of police officers by the public. I urge you to read this oath (as well as this book) several times as I promise you many of the questions you will be asked, will center around the philosophies contained in this oath.

Police Officer's Oath

As a Law Enforcement Officer, my fundamental duty is to serve mankind; to safeguard lives and property; to protect the innocent against deception, the weak against oppression or intimidation, and the peaceful against violence or disorder; and to respect the Constitutional rights of all persons to liberty, equality and justice.

I will keep my private life unsullied as an example to all; maintain courageous calm in the face of danger, scorn or ridicule; develop self-restraint; and be constantly mindful of the welfare of others. Honest in thought and deed in both my personal and official life, I will be exemplary in obeying the laws of the land and the regulations of my department. Whatever I see or hear of a confidential nature or that is confided to me in my official capacity will be kept ever secret unless revelation is necessary in the performance of my duty.

I will never act officiously or permit personal feelings, prejudices, animosities or friendships to influence my decisions. With no compromise for crime and with relentless prosecution of criminal, I will enforce the law courteously and appropriately without fear or favor, malice or ill will, never employing unnecessary force or violence and never accepting gratuities.

I recognize the badge of my office as a symbol of public faith, and I accept it as a public trust to be held so long as I am true to the ethics of the police service. I will constantly strive to achieve these objectives and ideals, dedicating myself before God to my chosen profession...law enforcement.

Made in the USA
Las Vegas, NV
25 November 2022

60311527R00056